I LIVE WITH DIABETES

WRITTEN BY CHRISTINA EARLEY

ILLUSTRATED BY
AMANDA HUDSON

A Starfish Book

SEAHORSE
PUBLISHING

Teaching Tips for Caregivers:

As a caregiver, you can help your child succeed in school by giving them a strong foundation in language and literacy skills and a desire to learn to read.

This book helps children grow by letting them practice reading skills.

Reading for pleasure and interest will help your child to develop reading skills and will give your child the opportunity to practice these skills in meaningful ways.

- Encourage your child to read on her own at home
- Encourage your child to practice reading aloud
- Encourage activities that require reading
- Establish a reading time
- Talk with your child
- Give your child writing materials

Teaching Tips for Teachers:

Research shows that one of the best ways for students to learn a new topic is to read about it.

Before Reading

- Read the "Words to Know" and discuss the meaning of each word.
- Read the back cover to see what the book is about.

During Reading

- When a student gets to a word that is unknown, ask them to look at the rest of the sentence to find clues to help with the meaning of the unknown word.
- Ask the student to write down any pages of the book that were confusing to them.

After Reading

- Discuss the main idea of the book.
- Ask students to give one detail that they learned in the book by showing a text dependent answer from the book.

TABLE OF CONTENTS

I LIVE WITH DIABETES

Hi! My name is Dayce.

I am seven years old.

I live with my mom, dad, and brother.
I have three dogs and two cats.

I have diabetes.

I wear an **insulin** pump.

I eat meals that have healthy
carbohydrates, proteins, and
fiber. I limit sugary foods.

Diabetes is a **disease** that affects how the body uses **glucose**.

Glucose is a sugar that is the body's main source of fuel.

I ride the bus to school. I sit next to my friend Hamza.

We talk about our favorite baseball teams.

Reading is my favorite subject.
I like learning about different
people, places, and things.

Coach Mack makes P.E. fun with exciting games. I eat some extra carbohydrates right before gym to keep my insulin in check.

Lunch is always a turkey sandwich with whole wheat bread, grapes, and milk.

After lunch, Nurse Lily makes sure
that my pump gives me the right
dose of insulin.

15

I play baseball with the Red Hawks.

I would like to play on a Major League Baseball team when I grow up. What do you want to do when you grow up?

LEARN ABOUT DIABETES

What Is Diabetes?

Diabetes is a long-lasting condition in which the level of glucose in the blood is too high. A hormone called insulin helps move glucose from food into the body's cells. Type 1 diabetes, or juvenile diabetes, happens when the body does not make insulin. It is genetic. Type 2 diabetes happens when the body doesn't make enough insulin or doesn't balance levels of insulin well. Eating healthy and being active can help prevent and treat type 2 diabetes.

People with diabetes must test the glucose level in their blood throughout the day. This can be done by pricking a finger and putting a drop of blood into a small machine called a glucometer. The machine lets the person know if they need to take insulin.

Another option is to use wearable technology. People with type 1 diabetes need to receive insulin on a regular basis. They must count the carbohydrates in their meals to adjust their dose of insulin. Then, a pump worn near the stomach can automatically give the right amount of insulin.

Although diabetes can be a lifelong condition, people who have it are able to live long and fulfilling lives by eating a well-balanced and healthy diet, exercising, and monitoring their insulin levels.

Websites to Visit

American Diabetes Association: diabetes.org

Beyond Type 1: beyondtype1.org

diaTribe Foundation: diatribe.org

Jerry the Bear: jerrythebear.com

Juvenile Diabetes Research Foundation: jdrf.org

Take the Pledge for Inclusion

☑   I accept people of all abilities.

☑   I respect others and act with kindness and compassion.

☑   I include people with special needs and disabilities in my school and in my community.

Get your parent's permission to sign the online pledge at PledgeforInclusion.org.

Famous People with Diabetes

Adele: Singer

Kris Freeman: Olympic skier

Tom Hanks: Actor

Nick Jonas: Singer

Charlie Kimball: IndyCar driver

Sonia Sotomayor: U.S. Supreme Court Justice

Adele

Charlie Kimball

Celebrate and Educate

American Diabetes Month happens in November.

World Diabetes Day is November 14th.

Inclusive Schools Week is the first full week in December.

WORDS TO KNOW

carbohydrates (kahr-buh-HYE-drates): sugar molecules found in foods such as bread, rice, and potatoes

disease (di-ZEEZ): an illness or condition that affects the body

dose (dohs): an amount of medicine taken at one time

glucose (GLOO-kose): a sugar that the body uses as fuel

insulin (IN-suh-lin): a hormone that regulates the amount of glucose in the blood

INDEX

COMPREHENSION QUESTIONS

1. Dayce wears ___.

   a. a leg brace

   b. an insulin pump

   c. glasses

2. Glucose is a kind of ___.

   a. sugar

   b. gas

   c. water

3. Dayce's favorite subject is ___.

   a. math

   b. reading

   c. art

4. True or False: Dayce eats lots of sugary foods.

5. True or False: Dayce plays baseball.

Answers: 1. b, 2. a, 3. b, 4. False, 5. True

ABOUT THE AUTHOR

Christina Earley lives in sunny south Florida with her son, husband, and rescue dog. She has been teaching children with special needs for over 25 years. She loves to bake cookies, read books about animals, and ride roller coasters.

Written by: Christina Earley
Illustrated by: Amanda Hudson
Design by: Under the Oaks Media
Editor: Kim Thompson

Photos: Tinseltown/Shutterstock: p. 21 (Adele); Grindstone Media Group/Shutterstock: p. 21 (Charlie Kimball)

Library of Congress PCN Data
I Live with Diabetes /Christina Earley
I Live With
ISBN 979-8-8873-5347-0(hard cover)
ISBN 979-8-8873-5432-3(paperback)
ISBN 979-8-8873-5517-7(EPUB)
ISBN 979-8-8873-5602-0(eBook)
Library of Congress Control Number: 2022948911

Printed in the United States of America.

Seahorse Publishing Company

www.seahorsepub.com

Published in the United States
Seahorse Publishing
PO Box 771325
Coral Springs, FL 33077